A SMALL DROP OF INK

Also by Linda Pendleton

Fiction:
The Unknown
Shattered Lens: Catherine Winter, Private Investigator
Fractured Image: Catherine Winter, Private Investigator
The Masquerading Cowboy, A Novella
Roulette by Don and Linda Pendleton

Nonfiction:
Three Principles of Angelic Wisdom
A Walk Through Grief
A Small Drop of Ink
Angelic Whispers of Love
To Dance With Angels by Don and Linda Pendleton
Whispers From the Soul by Don and Linda Pendleton
Metaphysics of the Novel by Don Pendleton, Linda Pendleton
Soul Expressions, Poetry Collection of Don and Linda Pendleton

E-Books:
A Loving Presence
The UFO Phenomena: The Cosmic SOS
How Thin the Veil! 150 Years of Spiritualism

E-Courses:
Journey to the Heart
Healing Whispers

Comic Adaptations:
The Executioner War Against the Mafia,
Don and Linda Pendleton
The Executioner Death Squad, Linda Pendleton

A SMALL DROP OF INK

A Collection of Inspirational and Moving Quotations of the Ages

Linda Pendleton

Pendleton Artists
California

Pendleton Artists
California

www.lindapendleton.com

Printed and bound in the United States of America by
Create Space
100 Enterprise Way
Suite A 200
Scotts Valley, CA 95066

This book is dedicated with love to my grandchildren,
Brian, Megan, Stephanie, and Daniel;
and to my great-nieces, Stephanie and Briana.
May each of you savor the wisdom of the past ages.
~L. P.

"God wove a web of loveliness
Of clouds and stars and birds,
But made not a thing at all
So beautiful as words."
–Anna H. Branch (1875–1937)

CONTENTS

INTRODUCTION

Words have great power and influence. We have been left a wealth of wisdom by the great minds of the past ages. Thousands of notable men and women have expressed their thoughts and ideas through poetry, speeches and literature. Those memorable thoughts have often changed the hearts and minds of mankind. The wisdom of the sages has inspired, motivated, and illuminated millions.

Many successful men and women have attributed their motivation and success to the words of a great thinker or orator. They may have been influenced by only a short quotation of someone's writing or speech. Perhaps just a few words, but ideas expressed that had a tremendous impact on their lives.

The power of words is dynamic, provocative, stimulating, and often, life changing. Words inspire, stir emotions, enable us to act or react. They give food for thought, and bring about new understanding and solutions to problems.

There are times when we may need inspiration to help us through the challenges, the self-doubts, the stresses, and the ups and downs of life. There are other times when we desire to be uplifted, invigorated, encouraged, to fill a thirst for knowledge, or to share in the expressed thoughts of others who have come before us.

Many of the great minds have been intellectuals, while others have been considered to be less. Some have been artistic and others not. Some were orators; others, deft with pen and paper. Still others were rebellious and passionate in their political or social views, while again, at the opposite extreme, were those of pacifistic or stoic natures.

Books such as the Bible, the sacred books of Buddhism, the Talmud, the Sayings of Confucius, and the Koran, are examples of writings that have shaped and influenced the lives of millions of people over the centuries. Words and ideas have ruled the world although, sadly, not always for the betterment of mankind.

I have always enjoyed quotations and have often used them as theme quotes within my books. Many of my favorite quotations come from the 19th century: an Age filled with gifted poets, writers, artists, philosophers, politicians, humanitarian movements, and spiritualism.

Many years ago, Lord Byron expressed my own sentiments well when he penned:

"Words are things; and a small drop of ink,
Falling like dew upon a thought, produces
That which makes thousands, perhaps millions think."

My collection herein of inspirational quotations barely scratches the surface of the wisdom of the ages. I have chosen inspirational quotations in six areas and have written a short piece for each section of the book. My choices of famous quotations, ancient and modern, are as relevant in today's world as they were when they originated.

I consider these quotations to be gifts for all of us. If even one quotation within this book makes you think about a problem in a new way, or makes you smile, gives inspiration, solace, or peace, or enables you to dream anew, then I have achieved what I set out to do in sharing these memorable quotations with you. Enjoy!

THE WONDERS OF NATURE AND BEAUTY

Over the centuries inspirational writers have penned beautiful poetry and prose regarding nature. It seems that too often our perceptions of the wonder and beauty of nature become somewhat clouded by everyday life and we fail to relish what nature has given us.

Children seem to have an innate curiosity about the wonder and magic of nature. But as we grow we often move away from that childlike curiosity. When was the last time you bent down on your knee to examine a tender green sprout that had recently broken through the rich brown soil and wondered how long it would be before it would become a beautiful wildflower? Have you often longed to see the barren winter turn toward early spring and bring forth the deep yellow of daffodils and soft pinks of tree blossoms?

As a child, did you ever look into a large puddle of fresh rain and wonder where the fish were? I did, many times. I would carefully examine rain puddles in my yard and be perplexed as to why there were not any fish swimming in the fresh water, nor tadpoles appearing who would one day soon, magically, turn into frogs.

I'm reminded of my youngest grandson, Daniel, when he was about three years of age, and his delight to discover tadpoles swimming in the shallow waters of a creek. I was tickled by his surprised response when he realized that tadpoles grew into small frogs such as the ones that were perched on the nearby rocks.

During childhood did you ever sing, "Twinkle, Twinkle, Little Star," as you gazed up to the glistening and sparkling stars and wonder if God had really put the millions and billions of stars in the heavens? How many times did you stand in the bright moonlight and study the "man" in the moon?

When I was about eight years of age, I spent time during the summer months with my grandparents. I recall a beautiful summer afternoon filled with songs of birds and flights of butterflies, colorful hues of zinnias, asters and snapdragons, aromas of ripe peaches, plums, onions, and tomatoes, and the lush green of zucchini and carrot tops. And I remember a treasure I discovered in my grandfather's garden—a cocoon.

I had carefully removed a portion of a twig and examined the thin thread of silk that attached the cocoon to the twig and I marveled. I found a small box in which to put my treasure and took it into the privacy of my guest room where I placed it on the window sill between the window and screen. Over the next few days I waited in anticipation for the upcoming event. One afternoon it happened. A funny little creature began to emerge, leaving behind the old, unfolding into a new existence, bringing forth a delicate beauty and brilliance of color, a life beginning anew.

At about that time my grandfather walked into the room and my immediate thought was that he might be angry that I had brought an insect into the house. I set aside my anxiety and told him, "Look, Papa, it's a butterfly."

He bent down to see and I gasped as his hand moved toward the box. Oh, no, Papa, don't hurt him! But before I could articulate my fear my grandfather put his index finger to the butterfly and the butterfly moved onto it.

"It's beautiful," he said.

I was a touch embarrassed for doubting his intentions. I knew better. Papa was a kind man and had an appreciation for nature. His beautiful garden, and the care he gave it, confirmed that.

He asked, "Are you going to keep him?"

I replied thoughtfully, "Only for a little while. I have to let him go soon, don't I?"

Even though I let the butterfly return to the wild of nature, I think of it every time I see a beautiful black and yellow Swallowtail butterfly flitting through my yard. At that time I also think of Papa.

Have you ever stood on the crest of a pine mountain top and gazed across the large expanse of a fertile valley below? Or encountered a beautiful waterfall cascading on the rocks? Have you stood at the bottom of a waterfall, invigorated by the cool mist of fresh water on your skin?

When was the last time the ocean brought rhythmic music to your ears while you watched the iridescent, glistening rays of the setting sun dancing across the water?

How long has it been since you climbed the branches of a large oak tree to peek inside a robin's nest, or stood in the falling snow and listened to the absolute silence?

Can you recall your first garden and your excitement and satisfaction the time you pulled your first carrot from the ground and took a bite, oblivious to the dirt stuck to it?

Take time to smell the roses. Do we take enough time from our busy lives to appreciate

and enjoy nature? Probably not often enough. It seems we take much for granted and fail to stop, to look, and appreciate. There is such beauty all around and it comes in varied shapes and forms. What a treat it can be to bring forward even a small piece of that beauty in all that we encounter. Life is marvelous. There is wonder, mystery, and beauty, eager to commune with us.

Nature is fragile. We need to be aware of what we are doing to our planet. It appears that many of our actions are destroying much of what nature has given us. We have to be consciously aware that we may be destroying that which cannot be replaced.

Of course, Mother Nature does give us our challenges from time to time: earthquakes, volcanoes, floods, hurricanes, blizzards, and other phenomena. We live on a vital and constantly changing planet–and it is all we have. We must take care of our beautiful blue planet, for our own benefit and for the benefit of future generations.

What better way to have reverence for our home planet than to appreciate and partake of the beauty of nature; to return once again to our childlike curiosity and wonder.

"My heart leaps up when I behold a rainbow in the sky."
–William Wordsworth (1770–1850)

"Come the spring
with all its splendor,
All its birds and all its blossoms,
All its flowers, and leaves, and grasses."
–Henry Wadsworth Longfellow (1807–1882)

"The clearest way into the universe
is through a forest wilderness."
–John Muir (1838–1914)

"What else is nature but God?"
–Seneca (4? B.C.–65 A.D.)

"Nature's laws affirm instead of prohibit.
If you violate her laws you are your own prosecuting
attorney, judge, jury and hangman."
–Luther Burbank (1849–1926)

"Beauty in things exist in the mind which contemplates
them."
–David Hume (1711–1776)

"Those things that nature denied to human sight,
she revealed to the eyes of the soul."
–Ovid (43 B.C.–17 A.D.)

"Each flower is a soul opening out to nature."
–Gėrard de Nerval (1808–1855)

"Nature is an unlimited broadcasting station,
through which God speaks to us every hour,
if only we will tune in."
–George Washington Carver (1864–1943)

"God is the friend of silence.
See how nature–trees, flowers, grass–grows in silence;
see how the stars, the moon and the sun, how they move
in silence...
We need silence to be able to touch souls."
–Mother Teresa (1910–1997)

"The moon like a flower
in heaven's high bower,
With silent delight,
Sits and smiles on the night."
–William Blake (1757–1827)

"Speak to the earth, and it shall teach thee."
–Bible, Job 12:8

"The stars are mansions built by Nature's hand,
And, haply, there the spirits of the blest
Dwell, clothed in radiance, their immortal vest."
–William Wordsworth (1770–1850)

"God moves in a mysterious way
His wonders to perform."
–William Cowper (1731–1800)

"Beauty is eternity gazing at itself in a mirror."
–Kahlil Gibran (1883–1931)

"I think that I
shall never see
A poem lovely as a tree."
–Joyce Kilmer (1886–1918)

"The book of nature is a fine and large piece of tapestry
rolled up,
which we are not able to see all at once, but must be
content to wait
for the discovery of its beauty and symmetry little
by little,
as it gradually comes to be more unfolded."
–Robert Boyle (1627–1691)

"How do you like to go up in a swing,
Up in the air so blue?
Oh, I do think it is the pleasantest thing
Ever a child can do!"
–Robert Louis Stevenson (1850–1894)

"A thing of beauty is a joy forever,
Its loveliness increases; it will never
Pass into nothingness."
–John Keats (1795–1821)

"The best and most beautiful things in the world
cannot be seen, nor touched...but are felt in the heart."
–Helen Keller (1880–1968)

"The universe is but one vast symbol of God."
–Thomas Carlyle (1795–1881)

"O beautiful for spacious skies
For amber waves of grain,
For purple mountain majesties
Above the fruited plain!

America! America!
God shed His grace on thee
And crown thy good with brotherhood
From sea to shining sea!"
–Katherine Lee Bates (1859–1929)

"How doth the little busy bee
Improve each shining hour,
And gather honey all the day
From every opening flower!"
–Isaac Watts (1674–1748)

"Die when I may, I want it said by those who knew me best, that I always plucked a thistle and planted a flower where I thought a flower would grow."
−Abraham Lincoln (1809−1865)

"There's a time each year that we always hold dear,
Good old summer time;
With the birds and the trees and the sweet scented breezes,
Good old summer time,
When your day's work is over then you are in clover,
And life is one beautiful rhyme."
−Ren Shields (1868−1913)

"The day is done, and the darkness
Falls from the wings of Night,
As a feather is wafted downward
From an eagle in his flight."
−Henry Wadsworth Longfellow (1807−1882)

"Little drops of water,
Little grains of sand,
Make the mighty ocean
And the pleasant land.
Little deeds of kindness,
Little words of love,
Make our world an Eden
Like the Heaven above."
–Julia Carney (1823–1908)

"I hold you here, root and all, in my hand,
Little flower–but if I could understand
What you are, root and all, and all in all,
I should know what God and man is."
–Lord Alfred Tennyson (1809–1892)

"Woodman, spare that tree!
Touch not a single bough!
In youth it sheltered me,
And I'll protect it now.
'Twas my forefather's hand
That placed it near his cot;
There, woodman, let it stand
Thy ax shall harm it not!"
–George P. Morris (1802–1864)

"Nature is a volume of which God is the author."
–William Harvey (1578–1657)

"When an apple tree's in blossom it is glorious
to see,
But that's just a hint, at springtime,
of the better things to be."
–Edgar A. Guest (1881–1959)

"Oh! the snow, the beautiful snow,
Filling the sky and the earth below!
Over the housetops, over the street,
Over the heads of the people you meet:
Dancing,
Flirting,
Skimming along
Beautiful snow! it can do nothing wrong."
–John Wittaker Watson (1824–1890)

"It is a wholesome and necessary thing for us to turn
again to the earth and in the contemplation of her
beauties to know of wonder and humility."
–Rachel Carson (1907–1964)

"Enflower the pathway of humanity with the beautiful
in life; plant gardens of love in unhappy bosoms."
–James Martin Peebles (1822-1922)

"Adopt the pace of nature:
her secret is patience."
–Ralph Waldo Emerson (1803–1882)

"Climb the mountains and get their good tidings.
Nature's peace will flow into you as sunshine flows into
trees.
The winds will blow their own freshness into you,
and the storms their energy,
while cares will drop off like autumn leaves."
–John Muir (1838–1914)

Linda Pendleton

"In your heart are birds and sunshine: in your thoughts
the brooklets flow:"
–Ralph Waldo Emerson (1803–1882)

"Down in a green and shady bed
A modest violet grew;
Its stalk was bent, it hung its head,
As if to hide from view.

And yet it was a lovely flower,
Its color bright and fair;
It might have graced a rosy bower,
Instead of hiding there.

Yet there it was content to bloom,
In modest tints arrayed;
And there diffused a sweet perfume,
Within the silent shade.

Then let me to the valley go,
This pretty flower to see,
That I may also learn to grow
In sweet humility."
–Jane Taylor (1783–1824)

"Old fashioned flowers! I love them all;
The morning glories on the wall,
The pansies in their patch of shade,
The violets, stolen from a glade,
The bleeding hearts and columbine,
Have long been garden favorites of mine;"
–Edgar A. Guest (1881–1959)

"What befalls the earth befalls all the sons of the earth.
This we know: the earth does not belong to man,
man belongs to the earth.
All things are connected like the blood that unites us all.
Man does not weave this web of life.
He is merely a strand of it.
Whatever he does to the web, he does to himself."
–Chief Seattle (1786–1866)

"Twinkle, twinkle little star,
How I wonder what you are!
Up above the world so high,
Like a diamond in the sky.

When the blazing sun is set,
When the dew is wet,
Then you show your little light,
Twinkle, twinkle, all the night."
–Jane Taylor (1783–1824)

"Who has seen the wind?
Neither you nor I;
But when the trees bow down their heads
The wind is passing by."
–Christina Rossetti (1830–1894)

"'Tis the last rose of summer,
Left blooming alone;
All her lovely companions
Are faded and gone."
–Thomas Moore (1779–1852)

"Look about, O what do I see?
O Spring, smiling at me–
Wake up, O pretty flower,
Spring has come, now is the hour!"
–Linda Pendleton (1942–)

"Sweet is the breath of morn, her rising sweet,
with charm of earliest birds."
–John Milton (1608–1674)

"The sun does not shine for a few trees and flowers,
but for the wide world's joy."
–Henry Ward Beecher (1813–1887)

"A light broke in upon my soul–
It was the carol of a bird;
It ceased–and then it came again
The sweetest song ear ever heard."
–George Gordon Byron (1788–1824)

"Silently, one by one, in the infinite
meadows of heaven,
Blossomed the lovely stars, the
for-get-me nots of the angels."
–Henry Wadsworth Longfellow (1807–1882)

"The west is broken into bars
Of orange, gold, and gray,
Gone is the sun, come are the stars,
And night infolds the day."
–George MacDonald (1824–1905)

"Nature herself has imprinted on the minds of all
the idea of God."
–Marcus Tullius Cicero (106–43 B.C.)

"I trust in nature for the stable laws
Of beauty and utility. Spring shall plant
And Autumn garner to the end of time."
–William Wordsworth (1770–1850)

"Flowers are God's divine bibles."
–James Martin Peebles (1822–1922)

"I found that when I talk to the little flower or
to the little peanut they will give up their secrets…"
–George Washington Carver (1864–1943)

"No town can fail of beauty, though its walks
were gutters and its houses hovels,
if venerable trees make magnificent colonnades
along its streets."
–Henry Ward Beecher (1813–1887)

"One touch of nature makes the whole world kin."
–Shakespeare (1564–1616)

"One is nearer God's heart in a garden
than anywhere else on earth."
–Dorothy Gurney (1858–1932)

"'Tis distance lends enchantment to the view,
And robes the mountain in its azure hue."
–Thomas Campbell (1777-1844)

"Those flowers made of light!"
–Thomas Hood (1799–1845)

"Reading about nature is fine, but if a person walks
in the woods and listens carefully,
he can learn more than what is in books,
for they speak with the voice of God."
–George Washington Carver (1864–1943)

"Wide flush the fields; the softening air is balm;
Echo the mountains round; the forest smiles;
and every sense and every heart is joy."
–James Thomson (1834–1882)

"Rain! whose soft architectural hands have power
to cut stones, and chisel to shapes of grandeur
the very mountains."
–Henry Ward Beecher (1813–1887)

"I believe a leaf of grass is no less than the
journey-work of the stars."
–Walt Whitman (1819–1892)

"How glorious a greeting the sun gives the mountains!"
–John Muir (1838–1914)

"A single sunbeam is enough to drive away
many shadows."
–St. Francis of Assisi (1181–1226)

"It is not so much for its beauty that the forest
makes a claim upon men's hearts,
as for that subtle something, that quality of air,
that emanation from old trees,
that so wonderfully changes
and renews a weary spirit."
–Robert Louis Stevenson (1850–1894)

"We are the stars and planets, the wind and the rain,
the sands and the seas–we, the miracles of creation,
are everything that has ever been."
–Don Pendleton (1927–1995), Linda Pendleton (1942–)

THE STRUGGLE
FOR FREEDOM AND EQUALITY

In 1776, our forefathers put together a document which appears to consider the fact that all Men are created equal and "endowed by their Creator with certain unalienable Rights, that among these are Life, Liberty and the Pursuit of Happiness." The unanimous Declaration of the Thirteen United States of America which seemed to grant these rights to all, obviously did not do that.

It has been a long and difficult road, spanning many years, for all Americans to achieve equality and personal freedom. Along that road, we had to endure the genocide of the Native American Indians, a peoples who lived on this land long before it began to be invaded by Europeans who decided to claim it as their own.

I recently discovered through my family genealogical research that my ninth great-grandmother, Penelope (Thomson) van Princes' life was saved by an American Indian by the name of Tisquantum, Chief of a Lenni Lenape tribe, members of the Algonquian language family and now known as the Delaware. The year was 1643. Penelope and her first husband, Kent van Princes, had sailed from their home in Amsterdam, Holland, across the Atlantic to the new world, planning to settle in the New Amsterdam area. The ship encountered a storm along our Eastern seaboard and made a landing on the rocky shoals near Sandy Hook, New Jersey. The recorded story is that Penelope's husband was deathly ill, and after the passengers made it to shore, the van

Princes couple were left behind while the other passengers departed for the New Amsterdam Dutch settlement of what is now New York City. The following morning, three Indians, described with feathers sticking up from coppery, shaved heads, attacked the couple. The husband, in a semiconscious state, was unable to defend in any way and was killed with one blow of a tomahawk. Penelope was brutally attacked, partially scalped, a knife wound to her arm, and a deep slash across her abdomen which exposed her bowels. The Indians left her to die there in the dense woods not far from the beach.

A strong and determined young woman, she somehow managed to hold her bowels in her abdomen and in grief and pain, lay there in a hollowed-out tree for seven days, surviving on tree sap and fungi. On the eighth day she was discovered by Tisquantum and a younger Lenape. Tisquantum carried her back to their village, and there she was nursed back to health using what I would consider to be Shamanistic Native American medicine. Chief Tisquantum, said to have been named for a noble ancestor, knew a little English, and asked Penelope to teach him more English during her recuperation.

In 1644, Penelope married Richard Stout and they had ten children. Penelope lived to be 110 years of age. She and Tisquantum remained friends until his death. A monument and commemorative coin have honored her in Monmouth, New Jersey. The coin depicts Penelope and Tisquantum.

After discovering this fascinating story of compassion, humanity, and friendship of two people of a different race and culture, I realized that I would not be here if this Lenape Native American had not saved the life of my ancestor. The discovery reinforces my belief that we are all connected.

Women were not granted full rights as citizens and it was in the early 1800's that women in this county became vocal. Their fight for equality broadened to include the abolishment of slavery prior to the outbreak of the Civil War. The devastating War Between the States, which resulted in the death of more than 600,000, often pitting brother against brother, father against son, neighbor against neighbor, former slave against slave owner, did not fully result in equality and freedom for the Black American.

Lincoln's Emancipation Proclamation was the beginning but man's inhumanity to man would continue for another one hundred years until the Civil Rights movement of the 1960's and beyond.

For women, also, the battle for equality continued for many, many decades. How often we forget that women, who have always been the strength behind the American family, were not granted the right to vote in this country until 1920.

Has man's inhumanity to man ceased? No. Thank goodness it has eased here in our country but bigotry and prejudice remain the mind set of some.

The battle for life, liberty, and the pursuit of happiness—and equality for all citizens of the United States of America—has been long and hard. Generation after generation, people have passionately fought to establish freedom and equality for all, no matter the color of skin, sex, religion, sexual orientation, physical disability, or social position.

It should be the hope of all of us that one day in the 21st century there will be an end to the horrific atrocities that have plagued the world, and that peace, freedom and equality will be in the minds and actions of all earth's inhabitants. It may be a hope and a dream that appears impossible—but what is life without a dream?

Harriet Beecher Stowe, author of the novel, Uncle Tom's Cabin, published in 1851-1852, was considered by many an abolitionist and Abraham Lincoln said of her, "the little woman who made this great war." She had stated that her internationally best-selling story, which portrayed the cruelties endured by an American slave family, came to her in a vision. Again, words have the power to change the world. Even if presented in a fictional format as done by Stowe.

It was Thomas Jefferson who said, "I like the dreams of the future better than the history of the past." So let's hang onto the dream that with each new day the world grows better.

"Those who deny freedom to others deserve it not for themselves,
and, under a just God, cannot retain it."
–Abraham Lincoln (1809–1865)

"Because man and woman are the complement of one another, we need woman's thought in national affairs to make a safe and stable government."
–Elizabeth Cady Stanton (1815–1902)

"Science may have found a cure for most evils, but it has found no remedy for the worst of them all–
the apathy of human beings."
–Helen Keller (1880–1968)

"Every man is free to do what he will,
provided he infringes not upon the equal freedom
of any other man."
–Herbert Spencer (1820–1903)

"Peace cannot be kept by force.
It can only be achieved by understanding."
–Albert Einstein (1879–1955)

"No one can make you feel inferior without
your consent."
–Eleanor Roosevelt (1884–1962)

"I leave you, hoping that the lamp of liberty
will burn in your bosoms until there shall no longer
be a doubt that all men are created free and equal."
–Abraham Lincoln (1809–1865)

"We all live with the objective of being happy;
our lives are all different and yet the same."
–Anne Frank (1929–1945)

"If the first woman God ever made was strong enough to
turn the world upside down all alone, these women
together ought to be able to turn it back, and get it right
side up again! And now they is asking to do it, the men
better let them."
–Sojourner Truth (1797–1883)

"The true republic: men, their rights and nothing more:
women, their rights and nothing less."
–Susan B. Anthony (1820–1906)

"A nation may lose its liberties in a day,
and not miss them for a century."
–Charles Montesquieu (1689–1755)

"The Lord Jesus defines the duties of his followers in his
Sermon on the Mount...without any reference to sex or
condition...never ever referring to the distinction now
being insisted upon between masculine and feminine
virtues. Men and women are CREATED EQUAL! They
are both moral and accountable beings and whatever
is right for a man is right for a woman."
–Sarah Grimké (1792–1873)

"The soul is free, and it is its freedom
that tells you every moment that you are free."
–Swami Vivekananda (1863–1902)

"There are two good things in life–
freedom of thought and freedom of action."
–W. Somerset Maugham (1874–1965)

"O sorrowing heart of slaves,
We hear you beat from far!
We bring the light that saves,
We bring the morning star;
Freedom's good things we
bring you, whence all
good things are."
–Algernon Charles Swinburne (1837–1909)

"Hope springs eternal in the human breast."
–Alexander Pope (1688–1744)

"Woman will always be dependant until she holds
a purse of her own."
–Elizabeth Cady Stanton (1815–1902)

"'A house divided against itself cannot stand.'
I believe this government cannot endure permanently
half-slave and half-free."
–Abraham Lincoln (1809-1865)

"I swear to the Lord
I still can't see
Why democracy means
Everybody but me."
–Langston Hughes (1902–1967)

"Above all, try to persuade your husband, father, brothers, and sons, that slavery is a crime against God and man, and that it is a great sin to keep human beings in such abject ignorance; to deny them the privilege of learning to read and write."
–Angeline Grimké (1805–1897)

"There will never be a generation of great men until there has been a generation of free women–
of free mothers."
–Robert G. Ingersoll (1833–1899)

"If you put a chain around the neck of a slave, the other end fastens itself around your own."
–Ralph Waldo Emerson (1803–1882)

"There never was a time when, in my opinion, some way could not be found to prevent the drawing of the sword."
–Ulysses S. Grant (1822–1885)

"Ideals are like stars: you will not succeed in touching them with your hands, but like the seafaring man on the desert of waters, you choose them as your guides, and following them you reach your destiny."
–Carl Schurz (1829–1906)

"You can't hold a man down without staying down with him."
–Booker T. Washington (1856–1915)

"I have a dream that one day on the red hills of Georgia, the sons of former slaves and the sons of former slave-holders will be able to sit together at the table of brotherhood."
–Martin Luther King, Jr. (1929–1968)

"It is never too late to give up your prejudices."
–Henry David Thoreau (1817–1862)

"Treat all men alike. Give them the same laws.
Give them all an even chance to live and grow.
All men were made by the same Great Spirit Chief.
They are all brothers. The earth is the mother of all
people, and all people should have equal right upon it."
–Chief Joseph (1840–1904)

"Give me your tired, your poor,
Your huddled masses yearning to breathe free."
–Emma Lazarus (1849–1887)

"The chief cause of human errors is to be found
in the prejudices picked up in childhood."
–René Descartes (1596–1650)

"Until you have become really in actual fact a brother
of everyone, brotherhood will not come to pass.
Only by brotherhood will liberty be saved."
–Feodor Dostoevski (1821–1881)

"A long time ago this land belonged to our fathers;
but when I go up the river I see camps of soldiers
on its bank. These soldiers cut down my timber;
they kill my buffalo; and when I see that,
my heart feels like bursting."
–White Bear (c. 1820–1878)

"Give to every other human being every right
that you claim for yourself–that is my doctrine."
–Thomas Paine (1737–1809)

"There is no more evil thing in this world
than race prejudice."
–H. G. Wells (1866–1946)

"The mystic bond of brotherhood makes all men one."
–Thomas Carlyle (1795–1881)

"Slavery is a flagrant violation of the institutions of
America–direct government–over all the people,
by all the people, for all the people."
–Theodore Parker (1810–1860)

"If I know my own heart it beats in accord with the
divine effort to better humanity, and throbs in tenderest
love toward all races and the people of all lands."
–James Martin Peebles (1822-1922)

"Let us all labor to add all needful guarantees for the
more perfect security of free thought, free speech, and
free press, pure morals, unfettered religious sentiments,
and of equal rights and privileges to all men, irrespective
of nationality, color, or religion."
–Ulysses S. Grant (1822–1885)

"In spite of everything I still believe people
are good of heart."
–Anne Frank (1929–1945)

"When you see your brother, you see God."
–St. Clement of Alexandria (c. 150–215)

"The land of the free and the home of the brave."
–Francis Scott Key (1779–1843)

"Dreams are the touchstones of our character."
–Henry David Thoreau (1817–1862)

"It is said that the colored man is ignorant, and therefore
he shall not vote. In saying this, you lay down a rule for
the black man that you apply to no other class of your
citizens. If he knows enough to be hanged, he knows
enough to vote. If he knows an honest man from a thief,
he knows more than some of our white voters.
If he knows enough to take up arms in defense of this
Government and bare his breast to the storm of
rebel artillery, he knows enough to vote."
–Frederick Douglass (1817?–1895)

"Hope is the thing with feathers
That perches in the soul
And sings the tune without words,
And never stops at all
And sweetest in the gale is heard."
–Emily Dickinson (1830–1886)

"Sometime they will give a war and nobody will come."
–Carl Sandburg (1878–1967)

"If you do not hope, you will not find what is
beyond your hopes."
–St. Clement of Alexandria (c. 150–215)

"Real human progress depends on a good conscience."
–Albert Einstein (1879–1955)

"Fourscore and seven years ago our fathers
brought forth on this continent a new nation,
conceived in liberty and dedicated to the proposition
that all men are created equal."
–Abraham Lincoln (1809–1865)

"I am a citizen, not of Athens or Greece,
but of the world."
–Socrates (479?–399 B.C.)

"I have never been able to conceive how any rational
being could propose happiness to himself from the
exercise of power over others."
–Thomas Jefferson (1743–1826)

"The measure of a man is what he does with power."
–Pittacus (650?–569? B. C.)

"It is a blessed thing that in every age some one has had
the individuality enough and courage enough to stand
by his own convictions."
–Robert G. Ingersoll (1833–1899)

"To correct the evils, great and small, which spring from
want of sympathy and from positive enmity among
strangers, as nations and as individuals, is one of the
highest functions of civilization."
–Abraham Lincoln (1809–1865)

"Even God cannot change the past."
–Agathon (447?–401 B.C.)

"I only ask to be free. The butterflies are free."
–Charles Dickens (1812–1870)

"In the gates of Eternity, the black hand and the white hand hold each other with an equal clasp."
–Harriet Beecher Stowe (1811–1896)

"Our true nationality is mankind."
–H. G. Wells (1866-1946)

"Governments exist to protect the rights of minorities."
–Wendell Phillips (1811–1884)

"Justice delayed is justice denied."
–William Ewart Gladstone (1809–1898)

"I think the first duty of society is justice."
–Alexander Hamilton (1757–1804)

"The spirit of truth and the spirit of freedom–
they are the pillars of society."
–Henrik Ibsen (1828–1906)

"Life has it ups and downs. When you are down,
the angels are waiting to lift you up."
–Linda Pendleton (1942–)

"I remember that all through history the way of truth
and love has always won. There have been tyrants and
murderers, and for a time they seem invincible. But in
the end they always fall. Think of this. Always."
–Mohandas Gandhi (1869–1948)

"Courage is resistance to fear, mastery of fear–
not absence of fear."
–Mark Twain (1835–1910)

"This land is your land, this land is my land,
from California, to the New York Island
From the redwood forest, to the gulf stream waters
This land was make for you and me."
—Woody Guthrie (1912–1967)

"There is nothing we cannot live down,
rise above, and overcome."
—Ella Wheeler Wilcox (1855–1919)

"For God hath not given us the spirit of fear;
but of power, and of love, and of a sound mind."
—Bible, 2 Timothy 1:7

"The opposite of love is not hatred, but indifference."
—Elie Wiesel (1928 –)

"Those who don't know how to weep with their whole
heart, don't know how to laugh either."
—Golda Meir (1889–1978)

"If a man does his best, what else is there?"
–General George S. Patton, Jr. (1885–1945)

"Now I say that with cruelty and oppression it is
everybody's business to interfere when they see it."
–Anna Sewell (1820–1878)

"Imagine there's no countries, it isn't hard to do,
nothing to kill or die for, and no religion too.
Imagine all the people, living life in peace."
–John Lennon (1940–1980)

"A *wounded* deer–leaps highest."
–Emily Dickinson (1830–1886)

"For whatsoever a man soweth, that shall he also reap."
–Bible, Galatians 6:7

"The world must be made safe for democracy."
–Woodrow Wilson (1856–1924)

"Never in this world can hatred be stilled by hatred;
it will be stilled only by non-hatred–
this is the law Eternal."
–Buddha (568–488 B.C.)

"The supreme art of war is to subdue the enemy
without fighting."
–Sun Tzu (c. Early 4th Century B.C.)

"None of us are born civilized, you know.
Gentleness is an acquired characteristic of our species,
not an inherent one. The civilizing process goes on and
the meek shall never inherit a savage earth.
The law of life simply won't allow it.
The meek need a champion if they are to survive."
–Don Pendleton (1927–1995)

"All violence, all that is dreary and repels,
is not power, but the absence of power."
–Ralph Waldo Emerson (1803–1882)

"Liberty is not in any form of government. It is in the
heart of free man; he carries it with him everywhere."
–Jean Jacques Rousseau (1712–1778)

"If we let things terrify us, life will not be worth living."
–Seneca (4 ? B.C.–65 A.D.)

"Many are the troubles of mankind."
–Aeschylus (525–456 B.C.)

"We should always be at war with injustice. Always."
–Maya Angelou (1928 –)

"To do injustice is more disgraceful than to suffer it."
—Plato (c. 428–348 B.C.)

"Ideals are like stars: you will not succeed in touching them with your hands, but like the seafaring man on the desert of waters, you chose them as your guides, and following them you reach your destiny."
—Carl Schurz (1829–1906)

"Only the just man enjoys peace of mind."
—Epicurus (371–270 B.C.)

"Wisdom consists in being able to distinguish among dangers and make a choice of the least harmful."
—Machiavelli (1469–1527)

"Be kindly affectioned one to another
with brotherly love."
—Bible, Romans 12:10

"The exterior man may be undergoing trials,
but the interior man is quite free."
−Meister Eckhart (1260−1328)

"Take precautions before the evil appears;
regulate things before disorder has begun."
−Lao-Tzu (c. 604−531 B.C.)

"The world is a looking-glass, and gives back to
every man the reflections of his own face."
−William Makepeace Thackeray (1811−1863)

"Our greatest glory consists not in never falling,
but in rising every time we fall."
−Oliver Goldsmith (1728−1774)

"If we could read the secret history of our enemies,
we should find in each man's life sorrow and suffering
enough to disarm all hostility."
−Henry Wadsworth Longfellow (1807−1882)

"All things change, yet we need not fear anything new."
–Marcus Aurelius Antoninus (121–180)

"Prudence is that virtue by which we discern what is
proper to be done under various circumstances
of time and place."
–John Milton (1608–1674)

"There is a remedy for every wrong and a satisfaction
for every soul."
–Ralph Waldo Emerson (1803–1882)

"Each one sees what he carries in his heart."
–Johann Wolfgang von Goethe (1749–1832)

"Into each life some rain must fall,
Some days must be dark and dreary."
–Henry Wadsworth Longfellow (1807–1882)

"Ring out the thousand wars of old,
Ring in the thousand years of peace."
–Alfred Tennyson (1809–1892)

"Nothing in life is to be feared.
It is only to be understood."
–Marie Curie (1867–1934)

"We all wear the golden threads that weave the divine
tapestry of existence...and we are forever one!"
–Don Pendleton (1927–1995), Linda Pendleton (1942–)

"I celebrate myself, and sing myself,
And what I assume you shall assume,
For every atom belonging to me as good belongs to you."
–Walt Whitman (1819–1892)

"But we do as a nation stand square on the doctrine
of liberty and justice for all."
–Francis Bellamy (1855–1931)

"All that is necessary for the forces of evil to win in the
world is for enough good men to do nothing."
–Edmond Burke (1729–1797)

"My country tis of thee,
Sweet land of liberty, Of thee I sing.
Land where my fathers died!
Land of the Pilgrim's pride!
From every mountain side,
Let freedom ring!"
–Samuel Francis Smith (1808–1895)

LIFE LESSONS

Have you ever wondered if life here on earth is an opportunity for lessons to be learned? In other words, is earth simply a school for learning? Are we here to have many, many experiences that allow us new spiritual understandings as we journey through life?

Surely, there is no denying that life gives us many challenges, many surprises, and lots of opportunity to learn from our misconceptions, our mistakes, or from our emotional reactions to events. It seems that spiritual and mental growth is the main objective of life. Of course, we may not always accept an experience or event as necessary to our growth. But the result, most often, is that we do learn more about ourselves after such life experiences.

We also learn from others as we observe how they move through events in their lives. Even with the most traumatic of occurrences, some are able to move quickly through the trauma and go on.

How do people achieve that? I believe it comes from an inner-strength that we all have. Often we are not aware that we do possess that kind of strength within us and we may not even discover it until we are put to the challenge of having to deal with some kind of devastating event. It is at those times that we must believe in ourselves and trust that we can indeed do what we need to do.

As we age, most of us can look back over our lives and recall the emotional reaction we may have had to an event and now realize that our reaction may seem to have been inappropriate. Was it inappropriate, or, for instance, were we then looking at our world through the eyes of a young child? Why would we expect the reaction of a child to have been any different than it was? We cannot now judge the reaction of that child we once were with our adult eyes. But how often do we do that to ourselves? Isn't it more logical to believe that in the past we were doing the best we could under the given circumstances, even with our immaturity, lack of world experience, irrational thinking, or even as the victim of abuse, real or imagined? The important thing to understand is that the past cannot be changed and when we hold onto it, it pulls us down and does not allow us the freedom to move forward with joy and passion.

If we have come into this life to experience certain lessons and to grow from these, are some of these lessons predestined, chosen by ourselves at a soul-level, to be experienced? Are these lessons part of our soul-growth? We can think of ourselves as a rose bud, which first begins as a small green nub and then begins to form the petals of a rose within. As the petals take shape and form, they evolve and grow, soon bursting open and revealing themselves to the world. And as the rose continues to grow, absorbing the rays of sunlight and soaking up nourishment which filters up from the roots of the rose plant, it continues its evolution, expanding, filling out, and maturing. It then becomes a beautiful, flourishing and thriving rose.

Life is growth, from our first helpless cry at birth to our last breath. Life is also a personal journey and we make our choices along the way, and observe our outer world in the way we choose. We also see our inner-world with our eyes alone. It is there in our inner-world where we shape who we are and project an image out to the world around us. We are many things and we change moment to moment as our perceptions change: perceptions of ourselves, as well as perceptions of the outer world. Life was meant to be that way. We are meant to grow, to learn, and to come to new understandings. That is our soul-purpose.

When I think about a long lifetime, I cannot help but think about my Aunt Loretta. She died in 1994, at the age of 97. She was a great example of living through change, personal traumas, and plenty of opportunity for growth. My aunt obviously was one of those people with an inner-strength. She also possessed a good sense of humor. I often saw her humor as a valuable trait for dealing with her life's many challenges. There was also her ability to grow with the times and to be accepting of the changes that had taken place in her lifetime over the full 20th century. She was like a rose, which blossomed and radiated its full brilliance.

If only we all could be so lucky to have resiliency, confidence, and humor about life. But is it really luck, or is it choice? Our choice?

"Learn to get in touch with the silence within yourself
and know that everything in life has a purpose."
–Elisabeth Kübler-Ross (1926–2004)

"The whole of life, from the moment you are born
to the moment you die, is a process of learning."
–Jiddu Krishnamurti (1895–1986)

"Heaven will be inherited by every man
who has heaven in his soul."
–Henry Ward Beecher (1813–1887)

"Imagination is more important than knowledge.
Knowledge is limited. Imagination encircles the world."
–Albert Einstein (1879–1955)

"Life is what we make it, always has been,
always will be."
–Grandma Moses (1860–1961)

"Sit in reverie and watch the changing colors of the
waves that break upon the idle seashore of the mind."
–Henry Wadsworth Longfellow (1807–1882)

"Most folks are as happy as they
make up their minds to be."
–Abraham Lincoln (1809–1865)
attributed to Lincoln by many

"Conscience is God's presence in man."
–Emanuel Swedenborg (1688–1772)

"I long to accomplish a great and noble task,
but it is my chief duty to accomplish small tasks
as if they were great and noble."
–Helen Keller (1880–1968)

"Time is
Too slow for those who Wait,
Too swift for those who Fear,
Too long for those who Grieve,
Too short for those who Rejoice,
But for those who Love
Time is not."
–Henry Vandyke (1852–1933)

"As a tale, so is life; not how long it is,
but how good it is, is what matters."
–Seneca (4? B.C.–65 A.D.)

"Patience is the companion of wisdom."
–Saint Augustine (354–430)

"The superior reasoning power...revealed in the
incomprehensible universe, forms my idea of God."
–Albert Einstein (1879–1955)

"God will not look you over for medals,
degrees or diplomas, but for scars."
–Elbert Hubbard (1856–1915)

"It is better to be a lion for a day than a sheep
all your life."
–"Sister" Elizabeth Kenny (1886–1952)

"The future belongs to those who believe in the beauty
of their dreams."
–Eleanor Roosevelt (1884–1962)

"Meditation is not a means to an end.
It is both the means and the end."
–Jiddu Krishnamurti (1895–1986)

"Some people are so afraid to die that they
never begin to live."
–Henry Vandyke (1852–1933)

"We are not human beings having a spiritual experience.
We are spiritual beings having a human experience."
–Pierre Teilhard de Chardin (1881–1955)

"You give but little when you give of your possessions.
It is when you give of yourself that you truly give."
–Kahlil Gibran (1883–1931)

"Leave nothing for tomorrow which can be done today."
–Abraham Lincoln (1809–1865)

"Faith furnishes prayer with wings,
without which it cannot soar to Heaven."
–St. John Climacus (525–600)

"Follow your bliss."
–Joseph Campbell (1904–1987)

"When one door of happiness closes, another opens;
but often we look so long at the closed door that we do
not see the one which has been opened for us."
–Helen Keller (1880–1968)

"It is my conviction that it is the intuitive, spiritual aspects of us humans–the inner voice–that gives us the 'knowing,' the peace, and the direction to go through the windstorms of life, not shattered but whole, joining in love and understanding."
–Elisabeth Kűbler-Ross (1926–2004)

"The soul should always stand ajar.
Ready to welcome the ecstatic experience."
–Emily Dickinson (1830–1886)

"Intuition will tell the thinking mind where to look next."
–Jonas Salk (1914–1995)

"So many gods, so many creeds;
So many paths that wind and wind,
While just the art of being kind
Is all the sad world needs."
–Ella Wheeler Wilcox (1850–1919)

Linda Pendleton

"Weeping may endure for a night, but joy
cometh in the morning."
–Bible, Psalms 30:5

"Live Large!"
–Don Pendleton (1927–1995)

"If something comes to life in others because of you,
then you have made an approach to immortality."
–Norman Cousins (1912–1990)

"I live for those who love me,
for those who know me true;
For the heaven that smiles above me,
and awaits my spirit too;
For the cause that lacks assistance,
for the wrong that needs resistance;
For the future in the distance,
and the good that I can do."
–George Linnaeus Banks (1821–1881)

"To love is to admire with the heart;
to admire is to love with the mind."
–Théophile Gautier (1811–1872)

"The great man is he who does not lose his child's heart."
–Mencius (372?–289?)

"Inspiration is universal. It over-swept with grandeur all
the past ages, and is just as fresh now as in time's earliest
morning. Poets, as much as prophets, are illumined with
a divine radiance. They think, they write and sing from
the very depths of their being."
–James Martin Peebles (1822–1922)

"Life is real! Life is earnest!
And the grave is not its goal;
Dust thou art, to dust returnest,
Was not spoken of the soul."
–Henry Wadsworth Longfellow (1807–1882)

"It is in our power to stretch out our arms and, by doing good in our actions, to seize life and set it in our soul."
–Origen (185?–254?)

"Our life is what our thoughts make it."
–Marcus Aurelius Antoninus (121–180)

"Our life is frettered away by detail...
Simplify, simplify."
–Henry David Thoreau (1817–1862)

"Do all the good you can,
By all the means you can,
In all the ways you can,
In all the places you can,
At all the times you can,
To all the people you can,
As long as ever you can."
–John Wesley (1703–1791)

"Learn from the past, be prepared for the future,
live in the present."
—Buddha (568–488 B.C.)

"I am the master of my fate;
I am the captain of my soul."
—William E. Henley (1849–1903)

"I never found the companion that was so
companionable as solitude."
—Henry David Thoreau (1817-1862)

"Happiness is a butterfly which when pursued is just out
of grasp... But if you will sit down quietly,
may alight upon you."
—Nathaniel Hawthorne (1804–1864)

"The human race has one really effective weapon,
and that is laughter."
—Mark Twain (1835–1910)

"Who has self-confidence will lead the rest."
—Horace (65-8 B.C.)

"Happiness, they say, is a state of mind,
but it is so much more. It is a state of being."
—Linda Pendleton (1942–)

"If a man does not keep pace with his companions,
perhaps it is because he hears a different drummer."
—Henry David Thoreau (1817–1862)

"But let me laugh awhile, I've mickle time to grieve."
—John Keats (1795–1821)

"Let me be a little kinder,
Let me be a little blinder
To the faults of those around me."
—Edgar A. Guest (1881–1959)

"We can't all be heroes because someone has to sit
on the curb and clap as they go by."
–Will Rogers (1879–1935)

"Man must cease attributing his problems to his
environment, and learn again to exercise his will–his
personal responsibility in the realm of faith and morals."
–Albert Schweitzer (1875–1965)

"Man's security comes from within himself."
–Manly Hall (1901–1990)

"Self discovery is a today function, a now,
a this instant thing."
–Don Pendleton (1927–1995)

"If you suffer, thank God!–it is a sure sign
that you are alive."
–Elbert Hubbard (1856–1915)

"We live in the midst of alarms; anxiety beclouds the
future; we expect some new disaster with each
newspaper we read."
–Abraham Lincoln (1809–1865)

"The strength of a nation is derived from
the integrity of its homes."
–Confucius (c.551–479 B.C.)

"...Or during the night when I cannot sleep, it is on such
occasions that my ideas flow best and most abundantly.
Whence and how they come I know not
nor can I force them."
–Wolfgang Amadeus Mozart (1756–1791)

"The mind is its own place, and in itself can make a
heaven of Hell, a hell of Heaven."
–John Milton (1608–1674)

"It better befits a man to laugh at life than
to lament over it."
−Seneca (4? B.C.−A.D. 65)

"Whenever two people meet there are really six people
present. There is each man as he sees himself,
each man as the other person sees him,
and each man as he really is."
−William James (1842−1910)

"A man who dares to waste one hour of time
has not discovered the value of life."
−Charles Darwin (1809−1882)

"It is a luxury to be understood."
−Ralph Waldo Emerson (1803−1882)

"There is nothing permanent except change."
−Heraclitus (540−475? B.C.)

"Trust people as if they were what they ought to be
and you help them to become what they are
capable of being."
–Johann Wolfgang von Goethe (1749–1832)

"All our knowledge has its origins in our perceptions."
–Leonardo da Vinci (1452–1519)

"Change your thoughts and you change your world."
–Norman Vincent Peale (1898–1993)

"Greatness lies not in being strong, but in the
right use of strength."
–Henry Ward Beecher (1813–1887)

"Nothing fixes a thing so intensely in the memory as the
wish to forget it."
–Michel de Montaigne (1533–1592)

"If you're not allowed to laugh in heaven,
I don't want to go there."
–Martin Luther (1483–1546)

"Make us happy and you make us good."
–Robert Browning (1812–1889)

"If I can stop one heart from breaking,
I shall not live in vain;
If I can ease one life the aching,
Or cool one pain,
Or help one fainting robin
Unto his nest again,
I shall not live in vain."
–Emily Dickinson (1830–1886)

"Judge a tree from its fruit; not from the leaves."
–Euripides (484–406 B.C.)

Linda Pendleton

"I know well what I am fleeing from but not what
I am in search of."
–Michel de Montaigne (1533-1592)

"Knowledge comes, but wisdom lingers."
–Alfred Tennyson (1809–1892)

"Hitch your wagon to a star."
–Ralph Waldo Emerson (1803–1882)

"To love oneself is the beginning of a lifelong romance."
–Oscar Wilde (1854–1900)

"Often the test of courage is not to die but to live."
–Vittorio Alfieri (1749–1803)

"Ask, and it shall be given you; seek, and ye shall find;
knock, and it shall be opened unto you."
–Bible, Matthew 7:7

"Do what you can, with what you have, where you are."
–Theodore Roosevelt (1858–1919)

"Man is what he believes."
–Anton Chekhov (1860–1904)

"There is no new thing under the sun."
–Bible, Ecclesiastes 1:9

"The great pleasure in life is doing what people
say you cannot do."
–Walter Bagehot (1826–1877)

"Lord, grant that I may always desire more
than I can accomplish."
–Michelangelo (1475–1564)

"Let us not burden our remembrance with
a heaviness that is gone."
–William Shakespeare (1564–1616)

"A good laugh is sunshine in a house."
–William Makepeace Thackeray (1811–1863)

"In every real man a child is hidden that wants to play."
–Friedrich Nietzsche (1844–1900)

"All the animals excepting man know that the
principal business of life is to enjoy it."
–Samuel Butler (1835–1902)

"Should you shield the canyons from the windstorms,
you would never see the beauty of their carvings."
—Elisabeth Kübler-Ross (1926–2004)

"The mind unlearns with difficulty what it
has long learned."
—Seneca (4? B.C.–65 A.D.)

"Our doubts are traitors
And make us lose the good we oft might win
By fearing to attempt."
—William Shakespeare (1564–1616)

"Knowledge is power."
—Francis Bacon (1561–1626)

"An idea, like a ghost, (according to the common nature
of ghost,) must be spoken to a little before it will explain
itself."
—Charles Dickens (1812–1870)

"You cannot please everybody, but to those souls who
cross you path, give kindness and love."
–Paramahansa Yogananda (1893–1952)

"Providence has given us hope and sleep,
as a compensation for the many cares of life."
–Voltaire (1694–1778)

"That best portion of a man's life,
His little, nameless unremembered acts
Of kindness and love."
–William Wordsworth (1770–1850)

"Beware of desperate steps!–the darkest days
Live 'tell to-morrow, will have passed away."
–William Cowper (1731–1800)

"Most men have more courage than even they
themselves think they have."
–Fulke Greville (1554–1628)

"Do not be too timid and squeamish about your actions.
All life is an experiment. The more experiments
you make the better."
–Ralph Waldo Emerson (1803–1882)

"A merry heart goes all the day,
your sad tires in a mile."
–William Shakespeare (1564-1616)

"When you have shut your doors and darkened your
room, remember never to say that you are alone,
for you are not alone, but God is within,
and your genius is within."
–Epictetus (c. A.D. 50–c.135)

"Better by far you should forget and smile,
Than that you should remember and be sad."
–Christina Rossetti (1830–1894)

Linda Pendleton

"Our care should not be so much to live long,
as to live well."
–Seneca (4? B.C.–65 A.D.)

"To live long, it is necessary to live slowly."
–Marcus Tullius Cicero (106–43 B.C.)

"The most utterly lost of all days, is that
in which you have not once laughed."
–Sebastien R. N. Chamfort (1741–1794)

"Man know thyself! All wisdom centers there."
–Edward Young (1683–1765)

"A light heart lives long."
–William Shakespeare (1564–1616)

"Examine the contents, not the bottle."
–The Talmud

"Neither fire nor wind, birth nor death,
can erase our good deeds."
–Buddha (563–483 B.C.)

"Always do right–this will gratify some and
astonish others."
–Mark Twain (1835–1910)

"A prudent question is one half of wisdom."
–Francis Bacon (1561–1626)

"Every artist dips his brush in his own soul,
and paints his own nature into his pictures."
–Henry Ward Beecher (1813–1887)

"We must accept life for what it actually is—
a challenge to our quality without which we should
never know of what stuff we are made,
or grow to our full stature."
–Robert Louis Stevenson (1850–1894)

"If we resist our passions, it is more due
to their weakness than our strength."
–Francois de La Rochefoucauld (1613–1680)

"Use what talents you possess: the woods
would be very silent if no birds sang there
except those that sang best."
–Henry Vandyke (1852–1933)

"One always has time enough, if one will apply it."
–Johann Wolfgang von Goethe (1749–1832)

"We must be willing to get rid of the life we've planned,
so as to have the life that is waiting for us."
–Joseph Campbell (1904–1987)

"To do nothing is sometimes a good remedy."
–Hippocrates (460?–370? B.C.)

"One of the greatest and simplest tools for
learning more and growing is doing more."
–Washington Irving (1783–1859)

"You cannot depend on your eyes when
your imagination is out of focus."
–Mark Twain (1835–1910)

"Man is always more than he can know of himself;
consequently, his accomplishments, time and again,
will come as a surprise to him."
–Henry Wadsworth Longfellow (1807–1882)

"Life is really simple, but we insist on making
it complicated."
–Confucius (c.551–479 B.C.)

"All things are difficult before they are easy."
–Thomas Fuller (1654–1734)

"Grief has limits, whereas apprehension has none.
For we grieve only for what we know has happened,
but we fear all that possibly may happen."
–Pliny the Younger (c. A.D. 62–c. 116)

"Be glad of life because it gives you the chance
to love and to work and to play and
to look up at the stars."
–Henry Vandyke (1852–1933)

"Ambition is so powerful a passion in the human breast,
that however high we reach we are never satisfied."
–Henry Wadsworth Longfellow (1807–1882)

"A kind heart is a fountain of gladness,
making everything in its vicinity freshen into smiles."
–Washington Irving (1783–1859)

"People are like stained-glass windows.
They sparkle and shine when the sun is out,
but when the darkness sets in, their true beauty is
revealed only if there is light from within."
–Elisabeth Kübler-Ross (1926–2004)

"You are the people who are shaping a better world.
One of the secrets of inner peace is the practice of
compassion."
–Dalai Lama (1935–)

"Where'er a noble deed is wrought,
Where'er is spoken a noble thought,
Our hearts in glad surprise
To higher levels rise."
–Henry Wadsworth Longfellow (1807–1882)

"It is in vain to expect our prayers to be heard,
if we do not strive as well as pray."
–Aesop (c. 6th century B.C.)

"A journey of a thousand miles must begin
with a single step."
–Lao-Tzu (c. 604–531 B.C.)

"Prayer is conversation with God."
–St. Clement of Alexandria (c. 150–c. 215)

"Certain thoughts are prayers. There are moments
when, whatever the attitude of the body, the soul
is on its knees."
–Victor Hugo (1802–1885)

"We have to deal, we have to feel,
and only then, can we heal."
—Linda Pendleton (1942–)

"As the soil, however rich it may be, cannot be
productive without culture, so the mind without
cultivation can never produce good fruit."
—Seneca (4? B.C. –65 A.D.)

"Give yourself more diligently to reflection;
come to know yourself."
—Epictetus (c. A.D. 50–c. 135)

"Our lives are songs; God writes the words
And we set them to music at pleasure;
And the song grows glad, or sweet or sad,
As we choose to fashion the measure."
—Ella Wheeler Wilcox (1855–1919)

"No bird soars too high, if he soars with his own wings."
–William Blake (1757–1827)

"As long as man stands in his own way,
everything seems to be in his way,
governments, society, and even
the sun and moon and stars."
–Henry David Thoreau (1817–1862)

"When everything is in its right place within us,
we ourselves are in balance with the whole work of God."
–Henri Frédéric Amiel (1828–1881)

"How blessings brighten as they take their flight."
–Edward Young (1683–1765)

"It is the passing shower that lets the rainbow appear."
–Francis Thompson (1859–1907)

"The ultimate value of life depends upon awareness,
and the power of contemplation
rather than upon mere survival."
–Aristotle (384–322 B.C.)

"We arrive at truth, not by reason only,
but also by the heart."
–Pascal (1623–1662)

"Our happiness depends on wisdom all the way."
–Sophocles (c. 495–406 B.C.)

"Truth is the only safe ground to stand upon."
–Elizabeth Cady Stanton (1815–1902)

"Such is the human race. Often it does seem such a pity
that Noah...didn't miss the boat."
–Mark Twain (1835–1910)

"Dignity does not consist in possessing honors,
but in deserving them."
–Aristotle (384–322 B.C.)

"The greatest griefs are those we cause ourselves."
–Sophocles (c. 495–406 B.C.)

"Keep what is worth keeping–
And with the breath of kindness
Blow the rest away."
–Dinah Mulock Craik (1826–1887)

"Sometimes one likes foolish people for their folly,
better than wise people for their wisdom."
–Elizabeth Gaskell (1810–1865)

"Therefore do not worry about tomorrow,
for tomorrow will worry about itself."
–Bible, Matthew 6:34

"Three things cannot be hidden, the sun, the moon
and the truth."
—Buddha (568–488 B.C.)

"No man ever prayed heartily
without learning something."
—Ralph Waldo Emerson (1803–1882)

"Be not forgetful to entertain strangers:
for thereby some have entertained angels unawares."
—Bible, Hebrews 13:2

"First say to yourself what you would be;
and then do what you have to do."
—Epictetus (c. 50–120)

"The best thing about the future is that it comes
only one day at a time."
—Abraham Lincoln (1809–1865)

"The important thing is not to stop questioning."
–Albert Einstein (1879–1955)

"A moment's insight is sometimes worth a life's
experience."
–Oliver Wendell Holmes (1809–1894)

"All that we see or seem,
Is but a dream within a dream."
–Edgar Allan Poe (1809–1849)

"The growth of the human mind is still high adventure,
in many ways the highest adventure on earth."
–Norman Cousins (1912-1990)

"What lies behind us and what lies before us
are small matters compared to what lies within us."
–Ralph Waldo Emerson (1803–1882)

"If you aspire to the highest place,
it is no disgrace to stop at the second,
or even the third."
—Marcus Tullius Cicero (106–43 B.C.)

"The work of an unknown good man has done is like
a vein of water flowing hidden underground,
secretly making the ground green."
—Thomas Carlyle (1795–1881)

"To be strong is to be happy."
—Henry Wadsworth Longfellow (1807–1882)

"The mind is the master over every kind of fortune;
it acts in both ways, being the cause of its own
happiness and its own misery."
—Seneca (4? B.C.–65 A.D.)

"It is not the style of clothes one wears, neither the kind
of automobile one drives, nor the amount of money one
has in the bank that counts. These mean nothing.
It is simply service that measures success."
–George Washington Carver (1864–1943)

"The entire whispering universe is at our beck and call.
Respond to it, interact with it, and you shall never,
ever feel alone again."
–Don Pendleton (1927–1995), Linda Pendleton (1942–)

THE POWER OF LOVE

One of the most powerful words in our language is the word, LOVE. It can also be one of our strongest emotions. The need to be loved and to love is a natural desire deep within our souls. We come into this world with a need and expectation that we will be loved unconditionally. We all desire love and the absence of love can bring pain and loneliness.

The dynamics of relationships, even from the child view, teaches us who we are. Are we lovable? Are we accepted? Do we have approval?

If we do not receive love, or fear that we may lose the love of others, we may then question our sense of self-worth. Don't we learn early on from social and emotional experience that love can be withdrawn based on how we behave or the reaction of others to us?

Just as important as having love is the ability to love others, and to love ourselves. From a spiritual perspective we may fear that we are separate, not part of a whole; alone, unloved, unaccepted. This feeling of separation is only an illusion, and when that is acknowledged, a merging with God, with self, and with others, takes place.

Love comes wrapped in many packages of different sizes, shapes, forms, intensities, conditions, and degrees of commitment. There is love between parent and child, love between mates, love of family, love of friends, and love encompassing the whole of mankind. And of course, there is the love of animals, our pets, which can be a very strong love bond.

It appears that unconditional love for all of life would be our highest achievement, and apparently, our greatest challenge to even come close to reaching that goal. But isn't it a nice thought and hope that each of us could come even a little closer to reaching that state of mind? Wouldn't it be beautiful if we could live in the kind of world where love ruled? But, obviously, it appears that we will have to wait to experience that type of existence until we are on the other side.

The traits of love—the essence of love—manifests with actions of compassion, understanding, approval, non-judgement, affection, encouragement, generosity, gentleness, to name a few.

Jesus preached, "Thou shalt love thy neighbor as thyself." Other spiritual teachers earlier than the time of Christ have also expressed that same message. Is that tenet our number one lesson as we journey through life?

"Take away love and our earth is a tomb."
–Robert Browning (1812–1889)

"Love is the only thing that we carry with us when we go, and it makes the end so easy."
–Louisa May Alcott (1832–1888)

"Love is doing small things with great love."
–Mother Teresa (1910–1997)

"Everything is bearable when there is love."
–Elisabeth Kübler-Ross (1926–2004)

"A true friend is the most precious of all possessions
and the one we take the least thought acquiring."
–Francois de La Rochefoucauld (1613–1680)

"Love has no other desire but to fulfill itself."
–Kahlil Gibran (1883–1931)

"We are all travellers in the wilderness of this world,
and the best we can find in our travels
is an honest friend."
–Robert Louis Stevenson (1850–1894)

"One word frees us of all the weight and pain of life:
That word is love."
–Sophocles (c. 495–406 B.C.)

"Love is a portion of the soul itself,
and it is of the same nature as it."
–Victor Hugo (1802–1885)

"It is only the souls who do not love
that go empty in this world."
–Robert Hugh Benson (1871–1914)

"How do I love thee? Let me count the ways.
I love thee to the depth and breadth and height
My soul can reach, when feeling out of sight
For the ends of Being and ideal Grace."
–Elizabeth Barrett Browning (1806–1861)

"Love is all we have, the only way that each can help
the other."
–Euripides (c. 485–406 B.C.)

"To live happily is an inward power of the soul."
–Marcus Aurelius Antoninus (121–180 A.D.)

"Your friend is that man who knows all about you,
and still likes you."
–Elbert Hubbard (1856–1915)

"The soul is not where it lives but where it loves."
–Thomas Fuller (1654–1734)

"A faithful friend is the medicine of life."
–The Apocrypha, 6:16

"No, there's nothing half as sweet in life
As love's young dream."
–Thomas Moore (1779–1852)

"Love is our highest word, and the synonym of God."
–Ralph Waldo Emerson (1803–1882)

"A friendship is a special, unique, state of being:
an entity readily identified
without resort to vows, spiritual or intellectual;
without recourse to sacraments,
dispensations, or decrees.
A friendship is a private thing.

A friendship is not a casual thing–
nor, indeed, is it a *thing* at all–
It is an essence, a *source* of things;
yet more than an idea,
much more than a suggestion,
and nothing at all like an inspiration–
A friendship is simply a movement, and a meeting,
and a recognition–within pure spirit."
–Don Pendleton (1927–1995)

"The well of life is love, and he who dwelleth
not in love is dead."
–John Tauler (1300–1361)

"Friendship is Love without his wings!"
–George Gordon Byron (1788–1824)

"There is nothing holier, in this life of ours,
than the first consciousness of love—
the first fluttering of its silken wings."
–Henry Wadsworth Longfellow (1807–1882)

"Love is the true means by which the world is enjoyed:
our love to others, and others' love to us."
–Thomas Traherne (1636–1674)

"With love our soul expands, and is enlarged with the greater life that attracts our affections, and is purified with its purity, and the soul goes forth out of herself, to live in the object of her love."
–William Bernard Ullathorne (1806–1889)

"If you would be loved, love and be lovable."
–Benjamin Franklin (1706–1790)

"Love possesses not nor would it be possessed;
For love is sufficient unto love."
–Kahlil Gibran (1883–1931)

"Love can never more grow old,
Locks may lose their brown and gold,
Cheeks may fade and hollow grow,
But the hearts that love will know
Never winter's frost and chill,
Summer's warmth is in them still."
–Eben Eugene Rexford (1848–1916)

"'Tis better to have loved and lost,
Than never to have loved at all."
–Alfred Tennyson (1809–1892)

"A true friend is one soul in two bodies."
–Aristotle (384–322 B.C.)

"We have been born to associate with our fellow-man,
and to join in community with the human race."
–Marcus Tullius Cicero (106–43 B.C.)

"All the kindness which a man puts into the world
works on the heart and thoughts of mankind."
–Albert Schweitzer (1875–1965)

"True goodness is loving your fellow man."
–Confucius (551–479 B.C.)

"If we would build on a sure foundation in friendship,
we must love friends for their sake rather than for
our own."
–Charlotte Bronte (1816–1855)

"Where there is love there is life."
–Indira Gandhi (1917–1984)

"Animals are such agreeable friends–
they ask no questions, they pass no criticisms."
–George Eliot (1819-1880)

"Kindness in words creates confidence.
Kindness in thinking creates profoundness.
Kindness in giving creates love."
–Lao-Tzu (c. 604–531 B.C.)

"The most terrible poverty is loneliness
and the feeling of being unloved."
–Mother Teresa (1910–1997)

"With love and patience, nothing is impossible."
–Daisaku Ikeda (1928–)

"The only way to have a friend is to be one."
–Ralph Waldo Emerson (1803–1882)

"By having a reverence for life, we enter into
a spiritual relation with the world."
–Albert Schweitzer (1875–1965)

"Owe no man anything, but to love one another."
–Bible, Romans 13:8

"Love conquers all."
–Virgil (70–19 B.C.)

"Keep love in your heart. A life without love is like
a sunless garden when the flowers are dead. The
consciousness of loving and being loved brings a warmth
and a richness to life that nothing else can bring."
–Oscar Wilde (1854–1900)

"The most I can do for my friend is to simply
be his friend."
–Henry David Thoreau (1817–1862)

"Love is a great beautifier."
–Louisa May Alcott (1832–1888)

"Love is the master key that opens
the gate of happiness."
–Oliver Wendell Holmes (1809–1894)

"To love and be loved is to feel the sun from both sides."
–David Viscott (1938–1996)

"Love is all we have, the only way we can
help each other."
–Euripides (c. 485–406 B.C.)

"Love dies only when growth stops."
–Pearl S. Buck (1892–1973)

"At the touch of Love, everyone becomes a poet."
–Plato (c. 428–348 B.C.)

"Love is the only gold."
–Alfred Tennyson (1809–1892)

"A new commandment I give unto you,
that you love one another."
–Bible, John 13:34

"Greater love has no man than this,
that a man lay down his life for his friends."
–Bible, John 15:13

"To love oneself is the beginning of a life long romance."
–Oscar Wilde (1854–1900)

"Love comforteth like sunshine after rain."
–Shakespeare (1564–1616)

"I awoke this morning with devout thanksgiving
for my friends, the old and the new."
–Ralph Waldo Emerson (1803–1882)

"Until you become really, in actual fact, a brother to
every one, brotherhood will not come to pass."
–Feodor Dostoevsky (1821–1881)

"You are part of the Infinite. This is your nature.
Hence you are your brother's keeper."
–Vivekananda (1863–1902)

"The divine principles–wisdom, love, truth."
–James Martin Peebles (1822-1922)

"The moment we exercise our affections, the earth is
metamorphosed; there is no winter, and no night;
all tragedies, all ennuis vanish–all furies even."
–Ralph Waldo Emerson (1803–1882)

"Love doesn't make the world go 'round.
Love is what makes the ride worthwhile."
–Franklin P. Jones (1887–1929)

"Two souls with but a single thought,
Two hearts that beat as one."
–Von Münch-Bellinghausen (1806–1871)

"Should auld acquaintance be forgot,
and never brought to mind?
Should auld acquaintance be forgot,
And days o'auld lang syne?"
–Robert Burns (1759–1796)

"Oh, it is sweet–it is life evermore
to breathe the beauty of love."
–James Martin Peebles (1822-1922)

"Home is where the heart is."
–Pliny (23–79)

"By the accident of fortune a man may rule the world
for a time, but by virtue of love he may
rule the world forever."
–Lao-Tzu (c. 604–531 B.C.)

"We are surrounded by eternity and by the uniting of
love. There is but one center from which all species
issue, as rays from a sun, and to which all species
return."
–Giordano Bruno (1548 ?–1600)

"Where love is concerned, too much is not even enough."
–Pierre-Augustin de Beaumarchais (1732–1799)

"Kindness gives birth to kindness."
–Sophocles (c.495–406 B.C.)

Linda Pendleton

"Wherever there is a human being there is
an opportunity for a kindness."
–Seneca (4? B.C.–65 A.D.)

"For in the sweetness of friendship let
there be laughter, and sharing of pleasures."
–Kahlil Gibran (1883–1931)

"I am wealthy in my friends."
–Shakespeare (1564–1616)

"Love is not merely a white lily undulating upon
embossed waters, not an æolean harp murmuring music
in the window, not the cooing of the turtle doves,
but an active principle, a divine soul emotion,
the central magnet of our conscious existence."
–James Martin Peebles (1822-1922)

"A friend may well be reckoned the masterpiece
of nature."
–Ralph Waldo Emerson (1803–1882)

"We have been friends together
In sunshine and in shade."
–Caroline Sheridan Norton (1808–1877)

"We're quite a pair, my dog and me,
Friends, companions we'll always be."
–Linda Pendleton (1942–)

"The ultimate lesson all of us have to learn is
unconditional love, which includes not only others
but ourselves as well."
–Elisabeth Kübler-Ross (1926–2004)

"So through the eyes love attains the heart;
For the eyes are the scouts of the heart,
And the eyes go reconnoitering
For what it would please the heart to possess.
And when they are in full accord
And firm, all three, in the one resolve,
At that time, perfect love is born
From what the eyes have made welcome to the heart."
–Guiraut de Borneilh (c. 1138-1200?)

"Where there is great love there are always miracles."
–Willa Cather (1873–1947)

"Love does not consist in gazing at each other
but in looking outward together in the same direction."
–Antoine de Saint Exupéry (1900–1940)

"My friends are my estate."
–Emily Dickinson (1830–1886)

"As you give love, you will have love."
–Alfred Tennyson (1809–1892)

"Love, I say, is the energy of life."
–Robert Browning (1812–1889)

"Love and compassion are necessities, not luxuries.
Without them humanity cannot survive."
–Dalai Lama (1935–)

"A loving heart is the truest wisdom."
–Charles Dickens (1812–1870)

THE CREATIVE DRIVE

The imagination is a powerful creative force and it springs from the self, although it may be stimulated from outside. Whenever the imagination is stimulated it looks for the proper vehicle to transport the expression outward. That expression can be conveyed through art, literature, music, invention, and in many other creative ways.

Artists often believe their inspiration comes from beyond–from the Muses. The ancient Greeks may have had something when they identified nine goddesses in the heavens who presided over literature and the arts and sciences. I have spoken with many artists and writers who often have had no idea where portions of their work have come from. Even though they may be typing the words, or holding the paint brush, they often are surprised by the words that end up on the page or by the brush strokes upon the canvas. They ofttimes joke and laugh about it but may know that their artistic expression came from elsewhere.

I recall a television interview I saw with author Taylor Caldwell in the late 1950's, in which she spoke about her novels and how she had no idea from where the detailed information she had written, had come. She has stated that she often had no technical knowledge of the subjects she wrote about. I was fascinated by her comment that often her fingers were guided at her typewriter and she considered it automatic writing. In later years I was to learn more about her writing process. That information was even more fascinating. She spoke of a Presence around her when she wrote and at times she would communicate with that Presence, receiving answers to her questions and information for the novel upon which she was working.

I have spoken with stone sculptors who have had nearly identical stories to tell. They see a chunk of stone and are shown what is "inside" it. And with that inspiration, they begin chipping away stone to reveal what they have been shown. Apparently Michelangelo was one of those sculptors who saw his work in that way and would chip away at the rock to reveal and set free the image inside. Again, fascinating.

Inspiration often comes through dreams. Many creative people have identified night dreams as revealing ideas, as well as day dreams. We've probably all had a problem to solve and have slept on the problem only to awaken with the answer. That seems to be a common event as our subconscious brings forward the answer. Another common experience is answers and ideas revealed during a shower or at the mirror shaving or applying makeup. Apparently during those times we quiet our mind and allow fresh thoughts to form.

As a writer and an artist, I have often wondered from where some of my ideas have originated. A few years ago I sculpted from clay a figure of a woman. It was my first experience working with clay. I found that as I built up and formed the clay it was almost as if the figure itself took on a life of her own and was guiding me. She is now cast in bronze but I have to admit I liked her better in the clay form as she seemed more alive and vital.

I would guess that many people yearn to be more creative. We often feel we do not have creative talent and that only successful painters, musicians, writers, and other artistic people are able to produce artistic works. But within each of us are powers of imagination and creativity waiting to be discovered, unleashed, and shared.

It seems that we think too often of creativity having to be some great masterpiece.

Creativity encompasses many things. I've mentioned the ones often thought of–art, literature, music, invention–but the list is much more extensive and possibly not as dramatic. It can be as simple as making a beautiful flower arrangement, cooking a gourmet meal served with elegance, crocheting a pair of baby slippers, decorating a room in your home, landscaping a yard, making a children's toy from wood. Many ordinary acts we do are creative and we do not always think of it in that way. Our simple accomplishments can bring us a sense of pride and satisfaction. And that satisfaction may not be any less than the satisfaction felt by a great master artist of the past.

"Imagination is the eye of the soul."
–Joseph Joubert (1754–1824)

"I dream my painting,
and then I paint my dream."
–Vincent van Gogh (1853–1890)

"Inspiration is an awakening, a quickening of all man's
faculties, and it is manifested in all high artistic
achievements."
–Giacomo Puccini (1858–1924)

"Creation is a drug I can't do without."
–Cecil B. DeMille (1881–1959)

"It is wise to learn;
it is God-like to create."
–John Godfrey Saxe (1816–1887)

"Our moments of inspiration are not lost though
we have no particular poem to show for them;
for those experiences have left an indelible impression,
and we are ever and anon reminded of them."
–Henry David Thoreau (1817–1862)

"Art is indeed not the bread but the wine of life."
–Jean Paul Richter (1763–1825)

"You must have chaos within you to
give birth to a dancing star."
–Friedrich Nietzsche (1844–1900)

"I begin with an idea and then it becomes
something else."
–Pablo Picasso (1881–1973)

"I hate flowers. I only paint them because they're
cheaper than models and they don't move."
–Georgia O'Keefe (1887–1986)

"The big artist keeps an eye on nature
and steals her tools."
–Thomas Eakins (1844–1916)

"There are always two people in every picture:
the photographer and the viewer."
–Ansel Adams (1902–1984)

"The artist never entirely knows. We guess.
We may be wrong, but we take leap after leap
in the dark."
–Agnes de Mille (1905–1993)

"Every artist dips his brush in his own soul,
and paints his own nature into his pictures."
–Henry Ward Beecher (1813–1887)

"The monotony and solitude of a quiet life
stimulates the creative mind."
–Albert Einstein (1879–1955)

"My ideas usually come not at my desk writing
but in the midst of living."
–Anais Nin (1903–1977)

"Who knows where inspiration comes from.
Perhaps it arises from desperation.
Perhaps it comes from the flukes of the universe,
the kindness of the muses."
–Amy Tan (1952–)

"Every good painter paints what he is."
–Jackson Pollock (1912–1956)

"The job of the artist is always to deepen the mystery."
–Francis Bacon (1561–1626)

"To have great poets, there must be great audiences."
–Walt Whitman (1819–1892)

"A work of art which did not begin in emotion is not art."
–Paul Cézanne (1839–1906)

"The key to the mystery of a great artist is that for reasons unknown, he will give away his energies and his life just to make sure that one note follows another inevitably...and leaves us with the feeling that something is right in the world."
–Leonard Bernstein (1918–1990)

"The aim of art is to represent not the outward appearance of things, but their inward significance."
–Aristotle (384-322 B.C.)

"Where the spirit does not work the hand, there is no art."
–Leonardo da Vince (1452–1519)

"Great art is the expression of a solution of the conflict between the demands of the world without and that within."
–Edith Hamilton (1867–1963)

"Everyone discusses my art and pretends to understand,
as if it were necessary to understand,
when it is simply necessary to love."
–Claude Monet (1840–1926)

"Artists in each of the arts seek after and care
for nothing but love."
–Marsilio Ficino (1433–1499)

"In art, the hand can never execute anything higher
than the heart can imagine."
–Ralph Waldo Emerson (1803–1882)

"Every production of an artist should be the expression
of an adventure of his soul."
–W. Somerset Maugham (1874–1965)

"The secret of art is love."
–Antoine Bourdelle (1861–1929)

"The essence of all art is to have pleasure in giving
pleasure."
–Mikhail Baryshnikov (1948–)

"Joy is but the sign that creative emotion is fulfilling
its purpose."
–Charles Du Bos (1882–1939)

"The man who never in his mind and thoughts
travel'd to heaven is no artist."
–William Blake (1757–1827)

"Art is not what you see, but what you make others see."
–Edgar Deges (1834–1917)

"You can't depend on your eyes if your imagination
is out of focus."
–Mark Twain (1835–1910)

"To create one's own world in any of the arts
takes courage."
–Georgia O'Keefe (1887-1986)

"Great art is an instant arrested in eternity."
–James Gibbons Huneker (1860–1921)

"Proper words in proper places make the true
definition of style."
–Jonathan Swift (1667–1745)

"Two most engaging powers of an author are to make
new things familiar, and familiar things new."
–Samuel Johnson (1709–1784)

"If any wish to write in a clear style,
let him be first clear in his thoughts;
and if any would write in a noble style,
let him first possess a noble soul."
–Johann Wolfgang von Goethe (1749–1842)

"Words–so innocent and powerless as they are,
as standing in a dictionary, how potent for good and evil
they become in the hands of one who knows how to
combine them."
–Nathaniel Hawthorne (1804–1864)

"There are two classes of poets–
the poets by education and practice, these we respect;
and poets by nature, these we love."
–Ralph Waldo Emerson (1803–1882)

"The greatest part of a writer's time is spent in reading
in order to write. A man will turn over half a library
to make a book."
–Samuel Johnson (1709–1784)

"How vain it is to sit down to write
when you have not stood up to live."
–Henry David Thoreau (1817–1862)

"Every author in some way portrays himself in his works,
even if it be against his will."
–Johann Wolfgang von Goethe (1749–1842)

"The writer is always working from his own individual
world view, whatever the subject, so an honest writer
cannot conceal himself in the work no matter how
hard he may try to do so."
–Don Pendleton (1927–1995)

"The pen is the tongue of the mind."
–Miguel de Cervantes (1547–1616)

"I lived to write, and wrote to live."
–Samuel Rogers (1763–1855)

"Either write something worth reading
or do something worth writing."
–Benjamin Franklin (1706–1790)

"The role of a writer is not to say what we all can say,
but what we are unable to say."
–Anais Nin (1903–1977)

"There is no greater agony than bearing an untold story
inside you."
–Maya Angelou (1928–)

"Most people never run far enough on their first wind to
find out they've got a second. Give your dreams all
you've got and you'll be amazed at the energy that
comes out of you."
–William James (1842–1910)

"A great book isn't written, it's rewritten."
–Phyllis A. Whitney (1903–2008)

"Words are potent weapons for all causes, good or bad."
–Manly Hall (1901–1990)

"I only wish I could write with both hands, so as not to
forget one thing while I am saying another."
–St. Teresa of Avila (1515–1582)

"A word is dead when it is said, some say.
I say it just begins to live that day."
–Emily Dickinson (1830–1886)

"If you wish to be a writer, write."
–Epictetus (c. 50-120 A.D.)

"Biting my truant pen, beating myself for spite;
Fool! said my Muse to me, look in thy heart and write."
–Sir Philip Sidney (1554–1586)

"True ease in writing comes from art, not chance,
As those move easiest who have learn'd to dance."
–Alexander Pope (1688–1744)

"The dignity of the artist lies in his duty of keeping
awake the sense of wonder in the world."
–Gilbert K. Chesterton (1874–1936)

"Music hath charms to soothe a savage breast,
To soften rocks, or bend a knotted oak."
–William Congreve (1680–1729)

"A great poet is the most precious jewel of a nation."
–Ludwig van Beethoven (1770–1827)

"Music is well said to be the speech of angels."
–Thomas Carlyle (1795–1881)

"Music is the universal language of mankind."
–Henry Wadsworth Longfellow (1807–1882)

"Every artist was at first an amateur."
–Ralph Waldo Emerson (1803–1882)

"Music is mediator between spiritual and sensual life."
–Ludwig van Beethoven (1770–1827

"O inspiration, from where do you come?
Tell me your secret, why so mum?
Did I write these words upon the page?
Or was it with help from a wise old sage?"
–Linda Pendleton (1942–)

"Music is the shorthand of emotion."
–Leo Tolstoy (1828–1910)

"Your art is as it were a grandchild of God."
–Alighieri Dante (1265–1321)

"Good art is nothing but a replica of the perfection of
God and a reflection of His art."
–Michelangelo (1475–1564)

"Ultimately, all writers long for the opportunity to share
their creation with the many. That is why most writers
write. But we also write because we *have* to. We have to
allow our creativity the avenue to find its proper *place–
expressed on the written page.*"
–Linda Pendleton (1942–)

"Unleash your creative power. Let it flow in all
its beauty."
–Don Pendleton (1927–1995)

WINDOWS OF THE SOUL

Our modern world would seem to be undergoing a strong re-identification with spiritual values and awareness. The re-identification can be noted by the growing public interest in a wide range of subjects such as angels and spirit guides, communication from the other side, spirituality, near-death experiences, reincarnation and past-lives therapy, the body-mind-soul connection, a holistic approach to healing, meditation and prayer, Oriental philosophy and medicine, self-empowerment, interpersonal and transformational psychology, and the list goes on and on.

The popularity of these various subjects, whether in literature, movies, television, seminars, or education, are representative of the re-awareness that is taken place among the general Western population. It appears in recent times that organized religion is not fulfilling spiritual needs of the modern world, so it should be no surprise that large numbers of people are seeking their spiritual connection in many ways, with some of the ways seeming not to be considered conventional by those of more conservative thought.

A recent poll indicates that 82% of Americans believe in an afterlife. The numbers are also increasing for those who believe they have had communication from a loved one on the other side.

It would seem that the religious instinct is innate within humankind, as though a template for the religious experience had been programmed into our genetic structures that govern human expression. Within the

128

innate religious or spiritual instinct are experiences that might be classified as miraculous. Are many of the events or experiences actually miracles or nothing more than ordinary occurrences?

Reports of extraordinary and astonishing events attributed to a supreme being or divine power will be found in virtually every world religion, culture, and probably within every human mind from primitive times right up into the modern age. Many cultures do not regard miracles or paranormal events as anything extraordinary but merely the natural workings of a natural world. Most cultures which share that idea have well-formulated spiritual beliefs that have been carried forward from generation to generation, throughout history, and many of these cultures have developed highly sophisticated belief systems.

When one reads the history of cultures, it is very apparent that there has always been a "knowing" within mankind that evolves into understandings that we are, indeed, spiritual beings and that life does not end with the death of the physical body. Mankind has always looked to the heavens in a search for answers. I have often wondered why that is and the answer I have come up with is that no matter our religious upbringing or belief system, we do, within us, have the knowledge that we are much more than a physical body having a life experience. We are temporarily using a physical body for an ongoing spiritual life.

When I look back at my life, I recall at a very young age knowing that there was more to life than just a few years we may have here on Earth. I have also been lucky to have experienced events that have convinced me beyond any doubt that life and love go on after the death of the body. I am hardly alone in that spiritual understanding. That idea and understanding has been presented in writings since the beginning of recorded history. We are also experiencing the convergence of science and spirituality and many in the medical profession are leading the way. Scientific studies are being conducted in various areas of life and death and maybe one day, in the not too distant future, there will be scientific evidence that consciousness lives on beyond the death of the physical body.

It is my hope that we are now coming into an age of new spiritual understanding where we can welcome and accept the gift of knowing that we are often given, no matter how subtle that gift may be. We are immortal, eternal spirits.

Those gifts not only make life more joyous, and grief easier, but help to remove the fear of death that has been placed culturally as an obstacle to spiritual growth and understanding. We do know who we are. We just have to bring that knowing, our remembrance, to the forefront. Increasing numbers of people are achieving that while in the body. And for those who do not rediscover the knowing, they will know without doubt one day as they pass into another state of being.

"I saw Eternity the other night
Like a great ring of pure and endless light."
–Henry Vaughan (1622–1695)

"When your friends begin to flatter you on how young you look, it's a sure sign you're getting old."
–Mark Twain (1835–1910)

"Death is not the greatest loss in life,
the greatest loss is what dies inside while we live."
–Norman Cousins (1912-1990)

"Vision is the art of seeing things invisible."
–Jonathan Swift (1667–1745)

"Joy comes, grief goes, we know not how."
–James Russell Lowell (1819–1891)

"Later I kept asking myself: 'What does it mean that my
father returns in dreams and that he seems so real?' It
was an unforgettable experience, and it forced me for the
first time to think about life after death."
–Carl Jung (1875–1961)

"To live in the hearts we leave behind,
Is not to die."
–Thomas Campbell (1777–1844)

"They are alive and well somewhere,
the smallest sprout shows there is really no death...."
–George Washington Carver (1864–1903)

"For visions come not to polluted eyes."
–Mary Howitt (1779–1888)

"Life is nothing but a journey to death."
–Seneca (4? B.C.–A.D.65)

"Our critical day is not the day of our death;
but the whole course of our life."
–John Donne (1572–1631)

"Long, long be my heart with such memories fill'd!"
–Thomas Moore (1779–1852)

"Life and death are two golden links in the chain of
endless being; demonstrating the goodness
of the Divine Existence."
–James Martin Peebles (1822-1922)

"There is another reality enfolding ours–
as close as our breath!"
–Don Pendleton (1927–1995)

"Our birth is but a sleep and a forgetting;
The soul that rises with us, our life's star,
Hath had elsewhere its setting,
And cometh from afar;
Not in entire forgetfulness,
And not in utter nakedness,
But railing clouds of glory do we come
From God, who is our home."
–William Wordsworth (1770–1850)

"Hush, my dear, lie still and slumber!
Holy Angels guard thy bed!
Heavenly blessings without number
Gently falling on thy head."
–Isaac Watts (1674–1748)

Linda Pendleton

"The boundaries between Life and Death are at best
shadowy and vague. Who shall say where one ends,
and the other begins?"
–Edgar Allan Poe (1809–1849)

"It is the secret of the world that all things subsist and do
not die, but only retire a little from sight and afterwards
return again. Nothing is dead."
–Ralph Waldo Emerson (1803–1882)

"Death is simply a disguised deliverance, or, like the
budding rose, it climbs up on the garden wall to bloom
on the other side."
–James Martin Peebles (1822-1922)

"At some future day it will be proved, I cannot say when
and where, that the human soul is, while in earth life,
already in an uninterrupted communication with those
living in another world."
–Immanuel Kant (1724–1804)

"Every moment of life is a step towards death."
–Pierre Corneille (1606–1684)

"The wise man looks not to how long he lives,
but to how he dies. For him death has no terrors,
because it is the day of his birth to immortal life.
And he will be mindful of those he has left behind,
and will commune with them."
–Seneca (4? B.C.–65 A.D.)

"Our fear of death is like our fear that summer will be
short, but when we have had our swing of pleasure,
our fill of fruit, and our swelter of heat, we say we have
had our day."
–Ralph Waldo Emerson (1803–1882)

"Oh, may I join the choir invisible
Of those immortal dead who live again."
–George Eliot (1819–1880)

"There is no death! The stars go down
To rise upon some fairer shore."
–John Luckey McCreery (1835–1906)

"What we have done for ourselves alone dies with us;
what we have done for others and the world remains
and is immortal."
–Albert Pike (1809–1891)

"Death is not extinguishing the light;
it is putting out the lamp because dawn has come."
–Rabindranath Tagore (1861–1941)

"The day which we fear as our last is but the birthday
of eternity."
–Seneca (4? B.C.–65 A.D.)

"For what is it to die but to stand naked
in the wind and to melt into the sun?...
And when the Earth shall claim your limbs,
then shall you truly dance."
–Kahlil Gibran (1883–1931)

"Life is the childhood of our immortality."
–Johann Wolfgang von Goethe (1749–1832)

"The nearer I approach the end, the plainer I hear
around me the immortal symphonies of the worlds
which invite me. It is marvelous, yet simple."
–Victor Hugo (1802–1885)

"The windows of my soul I throw
Wide open to the sun."
–John Greenleaf Whittier (1807–1892)

"There is a land of pure delight,
Where saints immortal reign;
Infinite day excludes the night,
And pleasures banish pain."
–Isaac Watts (1674–1748)

"In Heaven an angel is nobody in particular."
–George Bernard Shaw (1856–1950)

"I believe that a simple and unassuming manner of life
is best for everyone, best for both the body
and the mind."
–Albert Einstein (1879–1955)

"Heaven is under our feet as well as over our heads."
–Henry David Thoreau (1817–1862)

"Death is simply a shedding of the physical body
like the butterfly shedding its cocoon.
It is a transition to a higher state of consciousness
where you continue to perceive, to understand,
to laugh, and to be able to grow."
–Elisabeth Kübler-Ross (1926–2004)

"The bitterest tears shed over graves are the words
left unsaid and deeds left undone."
–Harriet Beecher Stowe (1811–1896)

"There is a land of the living and a land of the dead
and the bridge is love."
–Thorton Wilder (1897–1975)

"You don't have a soul. You are a Soul.
You have a body."
–C. S. Lewis (1898–1963)

"The grave is but a covered bridge
Leading from light to light, through a
brief darkness!"
–Henry Wadsworth Longfellow (1807–1882)

"Every mortal loss is an immortal gain."
–William Blake (1757–1827)

"What we once enjoyed we can never lose.
All that we love deeply becomes a part of us."
–Helen Keller (1880–1968)

"One often calms one's grief by recounting it."
–Pierre Corneille (1606–1684)

"If the doors of perception were cleansed
man could see everything as it is, infinite."
–William Blake (1757–1827)

"A man is not completely born until he is dead."
–Benjamin Franklin (1706–1790)

"Be of good cheer about death and know this as a truth–
that no evil can happen to a good man, either in life
or after death."
–Socrates (469–399 B.C.)

"To ease another's heartache is to forget one's own."
–Abraham Lincoln (1809–1865)

"The soul of man is immortal and imperishable."
–Plato (c. 428–348 B.C.)

"Life is a great sunrise. I do not see why death
should not be an ever greater one."
–Vladimir Nabokov (1899-1977)

"Triumphantly from star to star
He left the gates of Heaven ajar."
–Henry Wadsworth Longfellow (1807–1882)

"Is death the last sleep?
No, it is the last final awakening."
–Sir Walter Scott (1771–1832)

"I have absolutely no fear of death. From my near-death
research and my personal experiences, death is, in my
judgment, simply a transition into another kind
of reality."
–Raymond A. Moody (1944–)

"The act of dying is one of the acts of life."
–Marcus Aurelius Antoninus (121–180)

"While we are mourning the loss of our friend,
others are rejoicing to meet him behind the veil."
–John Taylor (1580–1653)

"For death is no more than a turning of us over
from time to eternity."
–William Penn (1644–1718)

"We sometimes congratulate ourselves at the moment of
waking from a troubled dream...it may be so at the
moment of death."
–Nathaniel Hawthorne (1804–1864)

"Nothing can happen more beautiful than death."
–Walt Whitman (1819–1892)

"Why fear death? It is the most beautiful adventure
in life."
–Charles Frohman (1860–1915)

"Life is eternal and love is immortal;
And death is only a horizon,
and a horizon is nothing save the limit of our sight."
–Rossiter W. Raymond (1840–1918)

"Each departed friend is a magnet that attracts us
to the next world."
–Jean Paul Richter (1763–1825)

"Do not take life too seriously.
You will never get out of it alive."
–Elbert Hubbard (1859–1915)

"God's finger touched him, and he slept."
–Alfred Tennyson (1809–1892)

"Earth has no sorrow that heaven cannot heal."
–Thomas Moore (1779–1852)

"In my Father's house are many mansions."
–Bible, John 14:2

"All religions must be tolerated...for every man
must get to heaven his own way."
–Frederick The Great (1712–1786)

"Angels are spirits, but it is not because they are spirits
that they are angels. They become Angels when they are
sent. For the name Angel refers to their office, not their
nature. You ask the name of this nature, it is spirit;
it is that of an Angel, which is a messenger."
–Saint Augustine (354–430)

"See how time makes all grief decay."
–Adelaide A. Proctor (1825–1864)

"Old age is like a plane flying through a storm.
Once you're aboard there's nothing you can do."
–Golda Meir (1898–1978)

"Heaven means to be one with God."
–Confucius (551–478 B.C.)

"Surely God would not have created a being as man
to exist only for a day!
No, no, man was made for immortality."
–Abraham Lincoln (1809–1865)

"What is human is immortal!"
–Edward Bulwer-Lytton (1803–1873)

"Don't you know who you are?
You are the greatest miracle ever produced
by the Universe.
You are. You exist. And you know that you exist.
That is the greatest miracle of all!"
–Don Pendleton (1927–1995), Linda Pendleton (1942–)

EPILOGUE

I have often been asked what my favorite quotes are. I have so many favorites that it is difficult to choose only a few. I believe my choice at any particular moment may depend on my frame of mind or mood. I may be looking for wisdom, inspiration, motivation, or comfort. Then again, there may be times when I read something that hits me at a deep level, words that resonate within me, touch me deeply, or even move me to tears.

I would say that the Lord Byron quote that I shared in the opening Introduction to this book, would be near the top of my list, as it really says it all about the power of the written word. It was for that reason that I chose a part of his quote for my book title. Again, the words of Lord Byron, penned many years ago:

"Words are things; and a small drop of ink,
Falling like dew upon a thought, produces
That which makes thousands, perhaps millions think."

The goal of the creative process is to move thoughts toward things so they can be experienced and shared by others. Thoughts become things when expressed. Words can produce vivid mental images. This quote does that for me. I see that small drop of black ink falling down upon a thought, and the ink allowing the words to be indelibly stamped into the mind of millions to experience. Some of the most enjoyable quotations are metaphors, literally a figure of speech in which a word or phrase that is ordinarily and primarily used to describe one thing or event is used to describe another. The metaphor provides color, harmonies, musical notes, symphonic results, and that allows for you to feel the words as they cascade through you. A way to emphasize that feeling is to read aloud. In doing so, the words magically move from a somewhat static form to one that comes alive with the help of vocal expression.

One can't help but wonder if English poet Lord George Gordon Byron (1788-1824) had any idea of the impact of his quote on future generations. Obviously, as a successful poet he probably had a good idea that his works would be enjoyed by future generations. What I find so interesting about a collection of famous quotes that spans centuries is that they are often as illuminating in today's modern world as they may have been when written or spoken.

Another quotation that is a personal favorite is this by Albert Einstein:

> "There are only two ways to live your life.
> One is as though nothing is a miracle.
> The other is as if everything is."

I chose to believe that everything is a miracle. I hope you do, too. It is also my hope that you find my collection a treasure and that you keep it beside your favorite chair or bedside and read it when you desire pearls of wisdom on such things as life, success, beauty, creativity and love.

ABOUT THE AUTHOR

Linda Pendleton has written in a variety of genres: nonfiction, novels, Comic book scripting, screenplays, and poetry. She coauthored several books with her late husband, renowned author Don Pendleton, including the popular nonfiction books, *To Dance With Angels; Whispers From the Soul;*, and the crime suspense novel, *Roulette: The Search for the Sunrise Killer.* She is author of *A Walk Through Grief, Crossing the Bridge Between Worlds; Three Principles of Angelic Wisdom, The Metaphysics of the Novel, the Inner Workings of a Novel and a Novelist* by Don Pendleton with Linda Pendleton; *The Cosmic Breath: Metaphysical Essays of Don Pendleton,* with Linda Pendleton. She has also co-written *Expressing Love: Remembering a Life* with psychotherapist Fred Bader, Ph.D.

Her fiction includes the *Catherine Winter Private Investigator* Series; *The Unknown*; and *Corn Silk Days, Iowa, 1862.*

Linda is a member of the Authors Guild. Several of her books have won awards. She enjoys family genealogy when not writing.

Learn more about Linda Pendleton at her web sites:
www.todancewithangels.com
www.lindapendleton.com